Me Too Movement

The #metoo Story

Lotti Davidson

Copyright © 2017.

All rights reserved. No part of this publication may be reproduced, distributed, or transmitted in any form or by any means, including photocopying, recording, or other electronic or mechanical methods, without the prior written permission of the publisher, except in the case of brief quotations embodied in critical reviews and certain other noncommercial uses permitted by copyright law.

This book is intended for informational and entertainment purposes only. The publisher limits all liability arising from this work to the fullest extent of the law.

Table of Contents

Introduction: A Global Viral Phenomenon

A Confluence of Factors

Unintended Consequences and Complications. What's Next, and the End Game

I. Introduction: A Global Viral Phenomenon

"*Me Too.*"

Two words managed to capture the desperately long history of harassment and violence exerted by abusive people in positions of power, against those they sought to dominate sexually. The victims were often women, but not exclusively. Sexual harassment and violence cut across gender, across age, across race, across professions and socio-economic status, across geography, across culture.

"*Me Too.*"

With just two words came a rallying cry for change. It showed the ubiquity and magnitude of a problem, and the urgency by which it should be addressed. Two words - as small as the first spark that lights a raging pyre, upon which would be thrown the old, oppressive order and from its ashes – a hope for change.

On one night in October, 2017, actress Alyssa Milano – a Hollywood fixture since her childhood years, best known for the long-running hit shows, *Charmed* and *Who's the Boss?* – was as absorbed as the rest of the population in the allegations of sexual assault against super producer Harvey Weinstein. A friend, Charles Clymer, sent her a screenshot that read, *"Suggested by a friend: if all the women who have been sexually harassed or assaulted wrote 'me too' as a status, we might give people a sense of the magnitude of the problem."* Milano thought it was a good idea, to shift the focus away from the acts of horrible men and toward the experiences of the survivors. She shared the screenshot with a caption of her own – *"If you've ever been sexually harassed or assaulted, write 'me too' as a reply to this tweet."*

It was evening of October 15th and she went to bed. She woke up to 55,000 replies and a no. 1 trending hashtag. The next few weeks would only add to that tally, with activity from 85 countries and millions of social media posts. The posts and shares could be simple and straightforward, with just the words "*#MeToo.*" Others felt compelled to expound on their personal experiences of sexual harassment and violence. Alyssa Milano never quite intended to do it, but she somehow lit a match and tossed it into an unexpected, global tinder. And the flames surged and spread.

#MeToo was used widely by countries with large English-speaking populations, like the United States, the United Kingdom, Australia and Canada, and was also used in India, China and Japan. It was "*#YoTambien*" en Espanol. It was "*#BalanceTonPorc*" in France – a call to 'denounce your pig.' In Italy, there was encouragement amongst survivors to speak openly about "that" time – "*QuellaVoltaChe*." The hashtag had been written out in Hebrew in Israel. It had a version in Arabic.

It only took a few days to show the magnitude of the problem and it was titanic, with a truly global scale.

The narrative shifted away from the fascinating spectacle of seeing a powerful man like Harvey Weinstein fall. He was just the tip of the iceberg. The problem was beneath; deep, wide-ranging and systemic. It wasn't just about one horrible man's alleged crimes; it was about the daily injustice women faced, which was so prevalent it did not even spare the most beautiful and wealthy people of the world. The narrative veered away from one man's egregious behavior, and instead shed light on how victims of sexual harassment had to deal with threats to their livelihoods; be coerced into silence; face skepticism, disbelief and worse, blame for what had befallen them; and live with the tolerance of the rest of society for the deplorable actions of powerful men. For a long time, there seemed no other recourse but to suffer silently. That is, until Alyssa Milano's accidental "movement."

Tarana Burke and "The me too Movement ™"

It is actually more accurate to say that the movement, accidental or otherwise, was not originated by Alyssa Milano. It was only reignited by her tweet.

#MeToo was popularized by the outspoken Hollywood actress, but its earliest use in its current purpose is attributed to sexual assault survivor and community organizer, Tarana Burke. She used "Me Too" all the way back in 2006 – over 10 years before the hashtag became a viral, rallying call for change against sexual harassment, abuse and violence.

Tarana Burke was born in The Bronx, New York in September, 1973. Life in a low-income household in the projects wouldn't have been easy for anyone, but she had also suffered rape and sexual assault when she was young. She found support in her mother, who reportedly encouraged her to find solace in community involvement. In this capacity, she became active in causes for young women of color, women from rough backgrounds, and sexual assault survivors.

Burke has been working toward social justice and the promotion of arts and culture in civil society organizations for over two decades. She was in the staff of the 21st Century Youth Leadership Movement; she was a consultant and special projects coordinator at the National Voting Rights Museum & Institute in Selma, AL; and spent time as Executive Director at the Black Belt Arts and Cultural Center, where she worked on programs for marginalized youth.

She would eventually go on to cofound her own organization. *Jendayi Aza*, born in 2003, was a program for girls of color, and it is this organization that would eventually morph into Just Be, Inc.

Just Be, Inc. was founded in 2006. The youth-oriented organization advocates for the health and well-being of young women of color in their teens and pre-teens. The advocacy is founded on the belief that these are especially vulnerable periods of growth, and that today's society offers plenty of pressure but little in the way of support for the unique experiences and challenges of women of color. The goal of the organization is to create solid foundations of esteem and self-empowerment that would equip these young girls with the ability to navigate around their circumstances and set a course for their own lives, helping them grow to become women of substance, strength and self-possession. As was noted in the JustBeInc. Website, "...*when all else fails they are equipped with everything they need to Just Be...*"

In the course of Burke's work with young women of color, sometime in the mid-1990's, she met a girl who would move her to begin the "me too Movement™." In the *JustBeInc.* website, Tarana Burke described the movement as being born from "*the deepest, darkest place in my soul.*" She wrote of how she had heard so many heartbreaking stories in her work, but the story of a young girl named Heaven was especially painful. She encountered Heaven at youth camp, where one of the activities was a bonding session where there was sharing of life stories. Burke listened and offered comfort, and left the girls with the reminder that they could approach adults like her if they wanted to talk more or had any other needs. The sweet-faced Heaven who sometimes acted out, took her up on that offer… only for Burke to come to the realization that she was ill-prepared for what Heaven was about to reveal.

Heaven was practically begging to be heard, and when Burke gave her time to speak, the adult couldn't even last more than a few minutes listening to Heaven's tales of abuse by her mother's boyfriend. Heaven shared her pain; Burke couldn't stand much of it. She sent Heaven to someone else to *"help her better,"* but she never forgot how Heaven's face showed rejection and closure. Burke confessed to thinking about that encounter often, because she let Heaven walk away to put her masks back on *"and go back into the world like she was all alone."*

Burke, in short, found that she did not have the courage, energy, or know-how to effectively comfort and connect on Heaven's level. She couldn't even say, *"me too."*

Thus, the "me too Movement ™" became a part of Burke's good work. Communities had to be better equipped in dealing with survivors of sexual abuse, assault or exploitation ("S.A.A.E."). The movement aimed to address the yawning gap between the needs of victims and currently available services, especially in underserved communities and communities of color. The movement also went beyond addressing rape and assault, and took on the nuances of "exploitation." It was, after all, also traumatic to be coerced into doing sexual favors, or to face severe and regular harassment even if neither types of sexual misconduct are overt situations of assault.

The goal was to impart a sense of empowerment and solidarity, and to remind young women that they were not alone in their struggles. Empathy therefore became a powerful tool because it combated shame and powerlessness on the part of victims. On a wider view, open sharing of these struggles also fought against society's silence and the normalization of what should otherwise be unacceptable behavior.

The realization of having a community is a precursor to personal healing, but also to social change. The program also includes training volunteers and advocates to help survivors cope.

Eventually, Burke and her team are looking at establishing a national hotline, a website with group and operator chat features, and providing education materials for schools, educators, communities and organizations. The materials will contain testimonies from survivors, kits on facilitating exchanges on SAAE, books and other resources.

The overarching vision was that of *"empowerment through empathy."*

"*Me Too"* was simple but deep, heartfelt and instinctively relatable. It resonated with SAAE survivors in the communities Burke worked in, just as it resonated with most women who encountered it when the hashtag became viral, even if they were unfamiliar with Tarana's vision or her good works.

The extent of the power of "*Me Too*" became apparent when it was fully unleashed… but first, it needed a confluence of factors to be truly heard and turned into the global phenomenon it eventually became.

II. A Confluence of Factors

The wide-ranging effects of the #MeToo movement are the product of thousands of years of history of women's struggles. A combination of factors turned it into an impactful phenomenon:

A. A shared understanding of what constitutes sexual misconduct;

B. A community that reminds sufferers they are neither alone nor powerless;

C. Cheap, accessible means of action;

D. The zeitgeist, usually triggered by key cases or incidents to rally around; and

E. Influence who are willing to champion the cause, including women in power, their "allies," and tireless, quality coverage from journalists to keep the conversation relevant and substantive.

In short, the #MeToo movement took off because a significant number of women knew that they were wronged or being wronged; because they realized they were not alone in suffering and thus able to voice, organize and pursue a common agenda; because technology and social media gave sufferers and their allies the means by which to pursue their goals; because it came at the right time, during an alleged misogynist's presidential term and a consequent resurgence in feminism, and while the Harvey Weinstein case was unfolding; and finally, people of power and influence who were willing to speak out, among them *Time* magazine's "Person of the Year" - "The Silence Breakers."

A. Evolving Perceptions of Sexual Misconduct

Sex is one of the world's oldest currencies. It's been given, withheld, traded, stolen, bought since time indeterminate. Sex and the desire for it – both welcomed and not - has long been a part of human existence. What may be surprising however, is that concepts and words for its forceful acquisition, as in the case of rape and other forms of assault or harassment, wouldn't come until relatively recently.

Historically, many societies conceived of raping women not as a crime against the person being assaulted but rather, a crime of property against the man who "owned" her. In the Bible – one of the world's oldest texts - wives were like houses, servants, and beasts of burden, in the sense that they were objects that the followers of God were discouraged from coveting. This can be found in The Ten Commandments, which is one of the most foundational elements of Christian faith, at Exodus 20:17: "*...thou shalt not covet thy neighbor's wife... nor anything that is thy neighbour's.*"

Adultery seemed to be a more conceivable notion; this, also a wronging against another man - the cuckolded husband. The laws around sex and assault could be really complex and sometimes convoluted. There were parts of the world that allowed a rapist's wife to be raped in turn by his victim's father; that required victims to marry their attackers; that assumed consensual premarital sex among two people if the woman did not scream – the consequence of which was stoning for both attacker and victim. Engagements between a raped woman and her husband-to-be could be broken off because she was considered damaged goods.

Among the earliest roots of the word rape is from the Latin *raptus* or *rapere* – nonsexual, forceful theft, as in the case of plunder and robbery. Its links to sexual violation would be firmer by the 1400s, but was still linked to theft. But it wasn't the theft of a woman's choices for her own body. In these instances, the underlying idea seemed to be that wrongdoing was committed not necessarily against the female victim, but against her male owner (as in her father or husband) and/or her community. As a matter of fact, even when it was considered a social ill, exemptions were legally or practically made (and yes, still continue to be made) on who "can" rape and who "can be" raped.

In war, women have been used as spoils, as in the "rape and pillage" of conquered territories. A fighting force, for example, may disapprove of rape within their own culture and communities, but not the opportunistic rape of the conquered for sexual gratification. Aside from women being considered as spoils of war, rape has also been "weaponized" in the sense that it had specific strategic goals and uses in warfare. In ethnic cleansing, systemic rape has been utilized to control the ethnicity of a population. The rape of an opposing or conquered group's women, who are traditionally conceived of as the nurturers of a community, have also been used as a tool for humiliation, intimidation and control.

In the late 1920s to the end of World War II, the Japanese forces were accused of using hundreds of thousands of "comfort women" in countries like China, Korea and the Philippines for military sexual slavery. Hundreds of thousands of women were raped in the 1970s during Bangladesh's battle for independence, as part of ethnic cleansing by opposing troops. In the 1990s, Serbian troops also used systemic rape toward ethnic cleansing in Bosnia. In Colombia, rival groups used rape and violence against women to control and punish communities. In short, whether or not rape was considered a crime or an ill within a community, the same restraint was not necessarily expected outside of it. A woman did not exist on her own, protected by her right to consent and decide. Her body was, again, to be violated or protected only in terms of her belonging to a man or to a group.

Apparently, conquered women, ethnically "undesirable" women, and women from opposition or rival groups "can" be raped. You know who else was allowed to rape for a long time? Husbands.

For a long time, it was believed that marriage meant permanent consent for sex and thus, a man couldn't legally rape his own wife. In the United States, it is widely regarded that the first convictions for spousal rape wouldn't come until 1979. If that feels recent, consider that spousal rape laws wouldn't be illegal in all states in the U.S. until the 1990s. If *that* feels recent, consider how then-Presidential candidate Donald Trump's former lawyer and aide, Michael Cohen, stunned the country when he said, "*You cannot rape your spouse.*" He would later apologize and disavow it as "*an inarticulate comment*" made in a heated exchange. Still, the apparent reckless comment was made in 2015.

Just like conquered women and strategically useful women, the protections accorded to a wife were not upon herself as a person *per se*, but upon the relationships she had with a man and with an institution – that of marriage.

You know who else "can" be raped? "Promiscuous" women. While it is well and right that the presumption of innocence is upheld for those accused of a crime as serious as rape and that, as the saying goes, 'it is better that 10 guilty men go free than an innocent one be condemned,' the justice systems of the world cannot seem to divorce these protections from victim-blaming.

In 1285, rape was subject to capital punishment in Medieval England… if only one could actually get a conviction from hesitant jurors who perceived of victims as agents of temptation. In 1736, jurist Sir Matthew Hale noted the difficulties of proving rape accusations from a woman with a not-quite "innocent" personal life… one of the earliest documentations of perceptions that still exist today, where the sexual history and lifestyle of a victim are commonly unearthed and dissected not just in the media and public discourse, but even by trained investigators and defense lawyers.

In the 19th century, a woman named Sylvia Patterson was raped in New York City by a Captain James Dunn. His charge? "*Assault with intent to seduce.*" The victim had accusations to face herself, however – she was called promiscuous, and it was alleged that she had venereal disease. Dunn was convicted... but with the all-too symbolic judgment of one dollar, it was apparent judgment was laid on Patterson's worth as a woman, too.

The enraging Brock Turner case of 2015 is a recent example. Turner, 20 years old and at the time a student athlete at Stanford University, was convicted of several felonies, including assault with intent to rape an unconscious, intoxicated woman, whom he had already sexually penetrated with a foreign object when two bystanders prevented him from causing her further harm. The incident happened by a dumpster outside a frat house after they met at a party.

The crime was traumatizing enough, but so were the questions that followed. The victim, "Jane Doe," fielded questions about her height and weight, her behavior at the party, her intent in drinking the amount of vodka that she did – "*You drank it all at once, right?... Like, chugged it? And that was a decision you made, right?*"

Appeals were made for the young man, saying he was already suffering from "*…a steep price to pay for 20 minutes of action…*" Turner's life, as described by his father, had "*altered forever*" and that "*His life will never be the one he dreamed about and worked so hard to achieve.*" He added that his son could be a positive contributor to society, with a commitment to "*…educating other college students about the dangers of alcohol consumption and sexual promiscuity.*"

What was missing from this line of thinking was the victim. When "Jane Doe" addressed the court, among her most powerful statements (which later also went viral online) was, "... *one night of drinking can ruin two lives. You and me. You are the cause, I am the effect...*"

Turner was given an outrageous sentence of a mere six months in jail. Judge Persky, who had handed out the sentence, cited Turner's lack of previous priors and positive character references as decision factors; "*A prison sentence would have a severe impact on him.*"

On *him*.

The victim was a shadow presence, a silhouette of a person, the object of '20 minutes of action.' This was a case where a young man was witnessed in action, and where the physical damages of assault were apparent and promptly reported and documented. But along the course of the trial, while the victim's individual decisions were considered, she was still looked upon based on her place within the norms set by society – how did she behave?

It wouldn't be the first time.

Survivors of assault often faced questions about what they were wearing, about whether or not they acted suggestively or in ways that could have been misinterpreted. They were asked about their drinking habits, about their sex and love lives, about whether or not they were "party animals." They were asked if they resisted or fought or asserted themselves and their denials more forcefully… It just never seems to be about the women's rights and entitlements on the simple merit of her existence. What did she do, what more could she have done – when the real perpetrator should not have done anything to hurt her, at all.

Words Have Power

If the word "rape" finds its origins around the 14th century, the phrase "sexual harassment" came into common use literally lifetimes later in America, in 1975. That does not mean that women haven't been subjected to unwanted sexual attention at their place of work, however. Pretty much as soon as women were in the workforce, lechery soon followed. Sexual coercion of female slaves and free domestic workers was common in the 18th and 19th centuries. By the time the 20th century rolled around and women were a part of the manufacturing and service industries, male supervisors could be just as abusive.

Complaining was unproductive; sufferers faced shame, skepticism, and/or belittlement of their concerns. It was all just part of working. It's not a big deal and happens to everyone. You should be flattered…

There seemed no other recourse but to suffer in silence or to quit… that is, until more and more women entered the workforce, and it grew increasingly unacceptable for sexual misconduct to be part of business-as-usual.

In 1975, Carnita Wood sought unemployment benefits from her former place of work, Cornell University. She left due to the unwanted attentions of a male supervisor and after Cornell's refusal to transfer her. Cornell stated she left for personal reasons; she and many other women felt vastly differently. Wood, along with Cornell University's

Human Affairs Office, founded Working Women United and engaged female workers from different backgrounds. There was harassment not only in the university but seemingly everywhere. The term "sexual harassment" popped up along the course of Working Women United's work, and was widely used after the *New York Times* used the phrase in an article.

To name something is to have power over it. It becomes something that can be described, identified, communicated to a community and thus, something that can be collectively championed or in this case, challenged. It can be prevented, codified into law and punished. Women working everywhere suddenly realized that what they were experiencing was neither isolated, nor acceptable. They had a cause to rally behind, and more concrete means of how to create change. What was oppressive but elusive tendrils of smoke that could not be grasped, became firmer, something one can combat and push back against.

'The Personal is Political'

Rape, sexual assault, sexual harassment, other sexual misconduct are all different things. If words have power, then certainly distinctions among them help in making them more defined and combatable. But underlying these deplorable actions is perhaps something more foundational – that victims, often women, are not being treated as equals. They are instead, property to be coveted. They are objects to be used. Levers to be pulled in war and conflict. 'They are 20 minutes of action.'

One viral post criticizes the approach of standing up for victims of sexual misbehavior by stating 'she is someone's daughter or sister or mom' or any other relationship. The argument should have ended with "*she is someone.*"

In feminist circles, the phrase "*The personal is political*" is important. What it basically boils down to is that what women go through in their personal lives – for example abuse or general discontent in their situations – can be traced to their political status and the larger inequality with which they have to live. The term was popularized by (though not originally attributed to) Carol Hanisch, who posited that personal experiences, such as those of women, are because of their place in the larger power system.

A woman who wants a fulfilling career, for example, may find discontent in the family and home burdens expected of her more than it is expected of her husband. A woman who is stuck in an abusive relationship, for example, may not have the means of escaping her situation. Perhaps she was being abused in the first place because she was perceived to be lesser; an object. Perhaps she did not have a viable job that would sustain leaving her abuser.

Under this frame of thought, the problems experienced by women behind closed doors seem to have systemic roots. Societal structures and context have to be examined too. With intricate patterns causing what at the outset may seem personal problems, escape therefore is not easy, and hardly ever a solitary affair. If a problem is not personal, then it will not be altered by personal efforts. Societal change requires organization and a louder voice.

B. The Power of Community

Even if one understood they were being wronged and how deeply entrenched and widely dispersed the problem was; even if one understood the consequent imperative for improvement – one does not necessarily feel empowered to change anything. This is where a sense of community comes in. Communities open discussions, share information, stoke inspiration and determination, and amplify the voices of individuals. After all, if personal experiences are rooted in political conditions, then the solutions may have to be political in nature too.

The Waves of Feminism

Women have historically organized around specific causes based on the context they were living in. The distinctions as they will be discussed here are basic, and still up for debate amongst scholars and the general public. But feminism, it's been said, comes in "waves" – generations, or eras with specific differentiating properties. These eras are not perfectly split apart without relation to other "waves," nor do they, like literal waves, crest and recede and rise again. It is, however, a compelling image that stuck in the lexicon since its use in the late-1960s as a loose framework of understanding the feminist movements and their most prominent (but not singular!) causes across history.

The First Wave is believed to have been around 1848 to 1920, marked by a political movement championing votes for women. The suffragettes pressed their case for years in lectures, protests and marches, facing ridicule and at times, even arrest and violence. It is interesting to note that amongst its most prominent organizers were women who were also active in the abolitionist movement; some of them fought not only for women's suffrage but also for universal suffrage. Many women of this wave looked upon the female vote as the first step that they had to make, in order to secure other rights.

The 15th Amendment was passed in 1870, which gave black men voting rights ahead of women. This caused an uproar from many in the feminist movement, and even unfortunately spurred racist reactions. Some white women found fury in "*field hands*" having more ability to influence the ruling of the country before "*educated women*." First-wavers fought on, however - for suffrage, for educational and employment opportunities, for their right to own property. Some of them started to look toward reproductive rights around this period too.

In 1920, the 19th Amendment finally gave women the right to vote. It was the banner achievement of the first-wavers, and its most unifying, specific and measurable objective. Women wouldn't find a cause as integral and unquestionable to rally around until years later.

The Second Wave is believed to have been from the early 1960s to the 1980s. Influential texts such as Simone de Beauvoir's *Second Sex* (released in the US in 1953), and Betty Friedan's seminal *The Feminine Mystique* (1963), were influential in the movement. One of the latter's most important insights was about "*the problem that has no name*" – a woman's general dissatisfaction with her home life, stemming not from their personal perceptions but from the systemic sexism that regulated and limited her roles and position in society.

Three million readers made Friedan's work a hit. Its sobering content sparked a movement for social equality, distinct from the voting rights championed in the previous wave. The phrase "*The personal is political*" became prominent in this period, and so, also political action and achievement. This era saw The Equal Pay Act; Title IX covering educational equality between men and women; reproductive rights via *Roe v. Wade*; the entrance of the phrase, "sexual harassment" into the common lexicon; and the prohibition of marital rape. They also combatted domestic violence through awareness and the establishment of shelters. The personal agonies of many women were now seeing systemic changes to challenge them.

Unfortunately, with the successes of oppressed women came threats to those who benefited from the system they meant to overturn. And with threats came backlash. Feminists were often portrayed as severe, unhappy, embittered, unattractive "bra-burners" who hated men – an image that is still linked to feminism today, even if it isn't properly representative of members of the movement.

The Third Wave? There is no consensus on the beginnings, endings, achievements or even the existence of a "Third Wave." Whether it is underway or over, however, there are some things that pundits do agree on. First, is that the Anita Hill case of 1991 was a part of it (whatever "it" was). She testified before the Senate that she had been sexually harassed in her workplace by then-Supreme Court nominee, Clarence Thomas (he would still go on to claim the seat). Her testimony led to a staggering number of sexual harassment cases. It also led to, in a sense, a national reckoning on the unfortunately limited role women played in governance. By 1992, over two dozen women won and made their places in the

Senate and the House of Representatives. The Anita Hill case unearthed some core characteristics of the Third Wave – to make the workplace a safe and productive space for women to thrive in, and to fight to have a larger slice of leadership.

In the most basic terms, The First Wave fought to be treated like human beings entitled to vote, education and property. The Second Wave fought to be viewed and treated on equal footing with men, in terms of pay, opportunities and societal expectations. The bra-burning image is seared here. The Third Wave relished in femininity and how they were distinct from men but no less able to hold leadership positions and make positive contributions to society. There was a more selective approach to the impositions of social structure, which they did not seek to completely upend. They welcomed, for example, high heels, makeup and yes, bras. There was recognition of pleasures to be found in some of their gender roles.

Speaking of appreciating the positive aspects of gender roles while fighting for equality, "The

Third Wave" was (*is?!*) also concerned with "intersections" with other oppressed sectors of society. This made them more inclusive to non-binary sexual orientations, like the plight of trans-people. This era is not marked by key legislative achievements, so that is probably why it is more amorphous, with an indistinct beginning and end.

The Fourth Wave? It seems premature at the onset to be discussing a fourth wave when the third is yet indeterminate, but this is where the current discourse puts #MeToo and similar movements, along with the women's marches on Washington and the record-setting number of females running for office partly as a backlash against the election of President Donald Trump. "The Fourth Wave" may even be a part of "The Third Wave," though it certainly seems as if it should be an entirely different era because of the distinctiveness accorded by technology. Technology underlies conversations, organization and action so comprehensively in this era, that many pundits argue this must be a separate wave altogether.

C. Technology

Evolving perceptions on what constitutes sexual misconduct led women to the knowledge that they were being wronged. Communities showed them they weren't alone, and organizations showed them it was possible to come together and create change. For the #MeToo movement, technology was the key enabler that spread information, began and facilitated conversations, and where political actions were planned, where these plans were disseminated, and where actions are documented and shared – which in turn provided more resources and information, spurred more conversations and inspired further action in a cycle that can keep going for a long time.

Resources includes feminist blogs and sites like *Jezebel*, *Feministing*, *Refinery29* and *Everyday Feminism*, which tackle a wide breadth of feminist issues alongside diverse interests including politics, pop culture, science, celebrity, beauty and wellness, with an infusion of intelligence and humor. Among the tools used for expression, community building and political action are Twitter and Facebook.

Petitions can be composed, signed and shared through functions like those offered by Change.org. Many feminist awareness campaigns and forms of community engagement have found life in these platforms.

While some campaigns seem to have taints of "slacktivism" – a shallow online activism that is characterized by ease of action, impulse and passion with little fact checking, quick to catch on but quick to burn out with little to no follow-through – online activism is indispensable in this day and age, and can be impactful in truly measurable ways.

"Raising awareness" and nurturing empathy and connection is of course important – #WhatWereYouWearing, #YesAllWomen and #YouOkSis showed that. But other sustained and well-organized campaigns have successfully put in and kept people from corporate or public office; have had staggering financial implications; and document and combat sexual crimes.

There are many examples of how feminist organizations harness the power of technology for change. The Women's Media Center tracks rape in Syria via a crowd-sourced map. Reebok dropped a brand ambassador whose lyrics showed rape culture, after a pressure campaign and petitions picked up steam. Public office hopeful Ken Cuccinelli got burned for policies that were not friendly to women via the "@KeepKenOut" Twitter handle, the "Keep Ken Out" website and a clever photo app that allowed users to insert him into scenes he did not belong in. The Representation Project used "#NotBuyingIt" to impact the advertising messages of companies who do not want to be the target of a boycott. The hashtag has also helped clear shelves (both digital and physical) of sexist content. Harrods and Disney, for example, have had to pull out such products due in considerable part to "#NotBuyingIt." "#StopRush" and the Stop Rush website cost the controversial TV host sponsorship revenues when he came after Georgetown law student Sandra Fluke in the wake of her testimony on birth control with incendiary and unjust comments.

Even Twitter and Facebook, which feminist organizations use to such great extent and effect, were not spared from their efforts. Feminist organizations and their supporters are responsible for keeping Twitter's "Block" function active (useful when prominent personalities in the movement are subject to online attacks), and for pushing Facebook to be more vigilant in policing inappropriate content.

D. The Spirit of the Times

Movements can find dizzying momentum when situated in a time ripe for change, is triggered by an event or series of events that are akin to 'the straw that broke the camel's back.' Suddenly, all the grievances of the past have ceased to become bearable. It can be thought of in terms of when a certain climate is conducive to a forest fire, and all it takes is a spark to begin a conflagration.

President Donald Trump

The loss of presidential frontrunner Hilary Clinton, one of the most qualified candidates to ever run for the highest office of the United States, was a painful moment for feminists and women in general, who ached to see a woman of Clinton's credentials become the first female to hold the position. That she had lost to Donald Trump – the caricature tycoon fond of gold everything, a boorish, intolerant bully, a reality TV star with a questionable history with women – was especially traumatic for them and for many Americans who did not support his vision for their country.

"The Resistance" against Trump came from different sectors of society. They crossed party lines and ideologies. There were feminists, the LGBTQ community, environmentalists, people of color, champions of diversity, and people who looked at Trump as unqualified, corrupt, and/or a threat to democracy, national security, free press and the due process of law. This so-called "resistance" had no leader, no structural organization, and no specific policy goals (where their more specific politics would have likely been divisive). The only thing that was clear? Vigorous opposition against President Donald Trump. In just one year of the controversial president's term, his actions have inspired well over 6,000 protests.

Women in particular wasted no time in conveying their profound disapproval. A Women's March was held as early the day after Trump's inauguration in January of 2017. It became the largest single-day mobilization in the history of the United States, with an attendance estimated at 3.2 – 5.2 million through a main march on Washington and coordinated marches held in different cities in the United States and in other parts of the world.

Donald Trump didn't really endear himself to women during the campaign (especially when the 'Grab them by the pu**y' tapes were released), and his performance during his first year in office did not really change anyone's perceptions of him. His critics found him to be a crass, sexist misogynist who objectified women. Before he was president, his antics were tolerated by society (even envied by some), and somewhat celebrated by entertainment media. But as a President, the mindset underlying his actions and statements became a real danger to the future of women not just in the United States but also abroad.

Trump's term has seen a decrease in international development aid providing women in vulnerable sectors of society with birth control, and he has also been a threat to reproductive freedom in the United States. The current administration was targeting coverage for contraception, as well as rules that impact discrepancies in the pay between genders. Planned Parenthood was put in the crosshairs. Presidential appointees slanted to the conservative, which threatened liberal policies and laws favorable to feminist causes. Furthermore, as the sexual misbehavior of prominent and powerful men were being let out into the sun by the voices of #MeToo, it may be recalled that Donald Trump's own list of accusers had earlier come into the public discourse (many women came forward with their tales after the decade-old *Access Hollywood* 'grab them by the pussy' tape was released in 2016). Trump's tally as of this writing is 20 women accusing him of misbehavior, harassment and even assault – including his then-wife Ivana (who used the word "rape" along the course of their divorce proceedings but has since walked back her statement); a former business associate; beauty pageant contestants; and contestants on his hit show, *The Apprentice*.

    The crushing loss of the presidency, an unapologetic public official exhibiting sexist and misogynist behavior sitting in the Oval office facing serious accusations of sexual misbehavior to boot, steering the country in a direction that can be described as counter to the needs of women… sounds bad enough. But society's tolerance and sometimes even celebration of pre-presidential Trump, and his eventual ascent to the highest office of the land in spite of his controversial statements and behavior, can perhaps be attributed to the toxic masculinity contemporary women have to live with every single day. It is a masculinity premised on control and domination, but is ironically often threatened by and oversensitive to emasculation, requiring aggressive assertion to maintain or regain. It is not just 'a feeling' either, or something benign, or a nuisance. It was truly dangerous.

A recent and extreme example of how toxic masculinity can have immediate, physical and wide-ranging danger is the case of Elliot Rodger, who left behind explanations why he went on a killing spree that ended with 14 injured, six dead, and his own life lost by his own hands following a mass shooting incident near the University of California, Santa Barbara. In his last video, he mentioned 'punishing girls' who for some reason, were never attracted to him – "*the perfect guy… the supreme gentleman.*"

Men are behind most of the mass shooting cases in the United States. And by most, we mean that since 1982, barely a handful were committed by women. Reasons cited for why these mass shootings keep happening vary – terrorism; inadequate gun control and a corrupt Washington dancing to the dollars of the gun lobby, say some; mental illness, say others. 'If there were *more* guns in the hands of good people, there would be less victims' has been mentioned too, as well as, simply, "*evil*." It is obviously an important question, and it really may be good to ask if unhealthy notions of masculinity may be playing a part in the situation, too.

Aside from Elliot Rodger's stranger-than-fiction, you-can't-make-this-stuff-up rants and explanations, many mass murderers, have a history of domestic violence too. Recent examples include Omar Mateen who killed 49 at the Pulse nightclub shooting; Robert Lewis Dear, who murdered three at a clinic for Planned Parenthood; and allegedly, Nikolas Cruz, who killed 17 school kids. These were men who were willing to use force and harm others to secure what they felt they were entitled to.

After Elliot Rodger's shooting spree and the revelation of his motivations, the hashtag #YesAllWomen became viral. It was in a response to the tragedy, and the sad defense of "Not all men" –

not all men were killers, not all men were abusers, not all men were rapists, not all men were violent, etc. The point of #YesAllWomen was that though not all men' were dangerous, the ubiquity of sexism and misogyny still compels 'yes, all women' to be hypervigilant in order to protect themselves. All women, it stated, had bad experiences and/or are reared to prepare to experience it.

The hashtag was used for stories like, hypervigilance against sexual crimes – like watching your drink at a party, and being ready to call 911 in case of an assault while walking home. It has been used to convey how women often needed to soften the blows of rejection, lest they court the anger and retaliation of a man – like giving out false phone numbers, or claiming to already have a boyfriend, instead of plainly conveying a lack of interest in a potential boyfriend. Or, as Margaret Atwood so artfully stated, "*Men are afraid that women will laugh at them. Women are afraid that men will kill them.*"

Trump of course, could not be blamed for these types of men. But this is the situation in the

America he ascended, the America that raised him up – and the America he was, by winning the presidency, charged with changing for the better. He wasn't quite up to the task, however, and he ultimately became a catalyst in reigniting the feminist movement. There had been male aggressions along the way, and Trump's presidency was like rubbing salt on a gaping wound.

Women have had enough.

The Harvey Weinstein Effect

Harvey Weinstein was an almost literal golden boy – his films have won 81 Oscars all together. Another specific measure of the producer's power in the entertainment industry is how many times he was thanked in an Oscar's acceptance speech. In an analysis of about 1,400 such speeches archived and available online, a study determined that he has been thanked more often than god, coming in second behind iconic director Steven Spielberg.

It would all come crashing down by October, 2017. A reckoning was afoot, not only for the gifted but flawed producer, but also for the industry that tolerated some semblance of his 'open secret;' other abusive men in powerful positions; and ultimately, for a world that has long lived with oppressive structures that allowed sexual predators to thrive.

Early that month, *The New York Times* published a story detailing the long history of Harvey Weinstein's alleged sexual misbehavior. Among those who broke their silence were well-known actors, Ashley Judd and Rose McGowan. The Weinstein Company launched an inquiry into the allegations and later booted him from the board of his own company.

The *New Yorker* magazine had additional tales to share too, and stories would soon be heard left and right of people finally willing and/or able to speak up against Weinstein. The list of accusers, including actresses both known and not-quite who have been the objects of Weinstein's alleged misbehaviors, grew. Soon, Oscar winners Mira Sorvino, Gwyneth

Paltrow and Angelina Jolie shared tales of harassment too. Accusations in a spectrum of horrors and crime snowballed, including those of Daryl Hannah, Salma Hayek, Uma Thurman, Oscar winner Lupita Nyong'o, *Game of Thrones'* Lena Headey, *Boardwalk Empire's* Paz de la Huerta and *The Sopranos'* Annabella Sciorra.

Accusations also came out about Weinstein damaging the careers of women who have denied or challenged him, or the careers of those they cared about. One of the most stunning claims is the possibility that Weinstein and/or his company may have gotten in the way of Oscar-winning filmmaker Peter Jackson's hiring of actresses Mira Sorvino and Ashley Judd for the groundbreaking, blockbuster *Lord of the Rings* trilogy.

Prominent male figures found voice to criticize the producer too – beloved actors like Tom Hanks, George Clooney and Leonardo DiCaprio, and even former United States President, Barack Obama.

The Cannes Film Festival, BAFTA and the Academy of Motion Picture Arts and Sciences, all scrambled to respond to the scandal against the decorated producer. By mid-month, Weinstein was expelled from the Academy. Before the year was over, he was stripped of his BFI Fellowship, banned for life by The Producers Guild of America and expelled from The Television Academy.

His actions soon became an object of investigations across the Atlantic, with legal actions underway in the United States and the United Kingdom. Weinstein lost the company that bore his name. He lost future work, as in the case of projects under development that suddenly came up for cancellation or review in light of the accusations against him. He lost his wife, Georgina Chapman. Eventually, he may lose his freedom, too.

E. Entertainment and Social Change

At this point, #MeToo had almost all the necessary ingredients for a viral phenomenon. Information, communities to turn to, technology to amplify its reach, and a charged climate ripe for a spark. Then came Hollywood.

Harvey Weinstein's alleged sexual transgressions cover a wide range of acts, including trading career advancement for sexual favors, forcing women to massage him, exposing himself, and rape and attempted rape. His most prominent victims were actresses, but they were not the only ones. Alleged victims included employees and work associates too.

But causes need rousing symbols and galvanizing voices. They need a face and inspiration. In this situation, a staggering number of known actors became just that. Well-known actresses not only broke their silence, they found support and courage in each other and found allies in prominent men in and out of the industry.

Entertainment can inspire change, there is nothing new about that. Its use as propaganda has a long history of proving so, from ancient civilizations kept happy by despots through theater and gladiatorial combat, to governments promoting humanity's long list of wars in wars in live performances and movies. But entertainment has also proven to be powerful in promoting social issues.

In Stanford University psychologist, Albert Bandura, PhD's social cognitive theory, people are able to learn from the behavior of their role models. This has seen action in "entertainment education" programs all over the world, for a variety of causes. Well-designed, compelling dramas can successfully push for specific social agendas.

Twende na Wakati in Tanzania managed to dispel misleading myths about HIV and AIDS in the 1990s; increase informed conversation about the disease; increase the practice of protected sex; and promote family planning – in the areas where the drama showed (versus where it did not, which experienced no such changes). Long before that, groundbreaking Mexican TV executive, Miguel Sabido was promoting social change via the hit *Ven Conmigo* in the 1970s, which dramatically increased enrollment rates in adult literacy programs. He would only improve over time, with a slew of educational hits in his country. Sabido magnified his impact by connecting with the nonprofit, Populations Communications International, and was thus able to share his techniques in other countries both directly through projects, and indirectly by example of showing what positive changes entertainment can do. Dramas all over the world have contributed to such causes as the promotion of education for women, an increase in the marrying age, family planning and birth control, HIV/AIDS awareness, adult literacy, and countless others.

In many dramas, the presentation is concluded by a short epilogue often done by a famous person, which summarizes learnings and may include points of action, for example a listing of health centers or other organizations where real-life sufferers can seek professional help.

Modeling and social learning – the positive power of celebrity in social action.

Characters of fiction can sow the seeds of change, and so could the actors who play them. This is why, in some parts of the world, the villains of film and television shows can face real-life public ire. This is also why, on a more positive note, celebrities are also used in the endorsement of products and the promotion of social causes. We've seen celebrities peddling shampoo, clothing and fragrances, just as we've seen them advocating for animal rights, fighting sex trafficking or as touring ambassadors for the United Nations.

After Harvey Weinstein, we saw them, alongside lesser known women, fighting against sexual harassment and inspiring people from all over the world, in all sectors of society, to do the same.

Time Magazine hailed "*The Silence Breakers*" as 2017's "Person of the Year." Ashely Judd, one of the first stars to speak up on the record about Weinstein, was recognized in the issue along with women from other industries standing up to their predators. The article also discussed the kinds of fears these different women had to overcome just to be able to speak out.

Actress Selma Blair spoke of a horrifying experience with filmmaker James Toback, who would even allegedly threaten her with harm unless she kept her silence. Encounters like this could leave sufferers in fear of their lives, just as Weinstein allegedly left aspiring actresses in fear for their careers if they spoke out. There were also existential fears. Some women, like the one who had helped change leadership at ride-sharing app Uber so drastically, did not want speaking out to define her identity. Multi-awarded, hit musician Taylor Swift was given a different moral issue to tackle – she was asked, on the witness stand in a trial unrelated to Harvey Weinstein, if she felt guilty about how her accusations got someone fired. The young woman's enlightened response? *"I'm being blamed for the unfortunate events of his life that are a product of his decisions..."* Swift was said to be motivated by the idea that if someone of her circumstances could be harmed thus without consequences, women at a more vulnerable position were more at risk.

They began, in the words of the magazine, *"a revolution of refusal."* They also began an era where women can encounter less skepticism when they make their accusations.

Up until the 1970s, women were suffering 'a problem with no name.' Eventually, problems like sexual harassment were articulated, but did not have a loud voice. 2017 helped to change that.

III. Unintended Consequences and Complications

There is no perfect movement, and the unintended consequences of their births can be both pleasantly surprising (like Milano's earth-shaking tweet), as well as unexpectedly horrifying. A 2000s TV actress tweets before bed for example, and she wakes up to a world afire with female unity and inspired action. But just as unintended, is the negative backlash from a multitude of fronts that followed from its success.

Before Harvey Weinstein: The Cases That Should Not Be Forgotten

There were already high profile cases of sexual predation in the workplace before the Harvey Weinstein scandal broke. Exposes and high level personnel changes were seen at Uber, as well as at

Fox News (which booted its top talent, Bill O'Reilly, and even chairman and CEO, Roger Ailes amid stories of sexual harassment). There were a staggering number of accusations against Bill Cosby.

In the less mainstream world of independent film, allegations against the industry's power players were making the rounds just before the Weinstein story broke – against Cinefamily's Hadrian Belove; writer Devin Faraci; and film geek extraordinaire, Harry Knowles. Some of these can get easily buried beneath the behemoth Weinstein scandal, especially as "After Weinstein" is fast becoming a marker of time in entertainment. The success of one movement can easily be the escape route of other predators, which is something that people may want to remember and be vigilant about.

After Harvey Weinstein: The Line Between Believing Women and a 'Warlock Hunt'

After the *New York Times* story broke and the scandal grew, it embroiled not only Weinstein himself, but also people who may have known about and/or looked the other way, which ultimately helped him stay in a position to continue his misbehavior. His company lost prestige, projects and revenues and is under threat of possible liabilities and bankruptcy.

Individuals like Amazon Studio's Roy Price for example, took a hit for allegedly ignoring actress Rose McGowan's allegations (on top of facing allegations of harassment himself). People who have worked with Harvey Weinstein and profited from their association with him faced backlash too, or struggled with their own consciences on the proper course of action to move forward. Filmmaker Kevin Smith, for example, of *Clerks*, *Chasing Amy* and *Dogma* fame, conveyed his devastation at his work being "*wrapped up*" in the horrors of Weinstein. He felt bad about how he had lionized Weinstein for a long time, "*...singing praises of somebody that I didn't f*cking know.*" He pledged to donate Weinstein-related residuals of his films, plus a fixed additional monthly sum for the rest of his life, for the empowerment of females working in the film industry. He shared his shame that "...*now I know while I was profiting, others were in terrible pain.*"

Aside from people with Harvey Weinstein connections, accusations against other powerful men in general emerged, among them, acclaimed actor Kevin Spacey, who would lose his hit Netflix show as well as be completely removed from a finished movie. British Defense Secretary, Michael Fallon, resigned from the Cabinet amid allegations of lunging after a journalist in 2003. Allegations came out against American politician Roy Moore. Senator Al Franken took a hit for inappropriate behavior too. Accusations emerged against Representative John Conyers, who resigned; and a sexual harassment settlement made by Representative Blake Farenthold (allegedly using taxpayers' money, too) was revealed in the media. Comedian and TV star Louis C.K. faced accusations of sexual misconduct, which forced him to re-examine consent within a power structure; "...*when you have power over another person,*" he had written, "*asking them to look at your d--- isn't a question. It's a predicament... I wielded that power irresponsibly...*" NBC's long-term *Today* show anchor, Matt Lauer, was fired for sexually inappropriate behavior. Chef, restaurateur and TV personality Mario Batali took a leave from work amid allegations of harassment. Acclaimed actor, James Franco, faced accusations; as did Jeremy Piven. The Metropolitan Opera's James Levine was fired amid evidence of sexual abuse... and so on.

Indeed, a long list of men faced a reckoning for a wide range of uncomfortable, inappropriate or downright criminal behavior. In music, there was a renewed interest in longstanding accusations against R&B hit maker, R. Kelly. A case was brought up against iconic Marvel king, Stan Lee. Accusations would be brought against NBC News' Tom Brokaw, CBS' Charlie Rose, TV host and producer, Ryan Seacrest, and actors, Morgan Freeman, Sylvester Stallone and Jamie Foxx. Fashion fixtures such as Guess co-founder Paul Marciano and photographers Patrick Demarchelier and Mario Testino are also taking fire, as well as bestselling author, Jay Asher of *Thirteen Reasons Why* fame. Las Vegas tycoon and

RNC finance chairman Steve Wynn is also feeling the heat, and so is fellow Vegas power player, the magician David Copperfield.

This is just a tiny slice of a very long list that is still growing, with cases that are still developing. If they are hard to keep track of, they must be near-impossible to follow through and prosecute. But that is one of the challenges of this complicated time.

Another challenge is whether or not #MeToo is crossing over to witch hunt – or, as one writer put it, "warlock hunt" levels. One of the situations where the question was raised is when a story came out on Babe.net about an anonymous woman's date with TV and movie star, stand-up comedian, Aziz Ansari. The unknown female was uncomfortable and communicated it, but the celebrity was persistent in his advances and she eventually gave in. He apologized to her for having *"misread things in the moment."* So was it really fitting to #MeToo, or "just" a bad date? Was it "just" a normal sexual interaction between a man and a woman? Even if it were "normal," is "normal" really equal between men and women to begin with? These are questions that society will have to grapple with. Apparently, we all understand sexual harassment to be bad, but where, really, are the lines that cannot be crossed?

Aside from the possible problem of mixed signals and blurred lines, the #MeToo campaign has increased the "believability" of women, which is of course, a good thing, but many are also rightly concerned of possible opportunists who may insert themselves into an otherwise empowering and positive narrative. This can harm not only the falsely accused, but have the wider-ranging effect of damaging the credibility of other women.

Is #MeToo a Step Back for Women in the Workplace?

Another concern about #MeToo is that it may be detrimental to women in the workplace.

Certainly the protection of women as they go about their daily lives in their place of work is an intrinsic good, but practically speaking, it has its pitfalls. For example, men in the lobbying industries may be afraid to meet privately with women. Lobbying firms and other similar industries may consequently be wary of hiring women, if they cannot be effective in securing meetings and conducting them because of the constraints of this changed sexual environment.

This is why some feminists fear the aggressive success of #MeToo, and how it can inspire some corners to return to an almost puritanical segregation of sexes in the workplace.

Has #Me Too Hijacked Tarana Burke's "me too Movement ™?"

Tarana Burke, the community advocate who founded "MeToo," rightly feared that her decade-long work would be drowned out by the dramatically more popular hashtag. In an interview, she described she felt she *"had to ring the alarm… before my work is erased…"* As the phrase became viral, however, she reconciled herself with the phenomenon; she (probably more than anyone else) knew the potential of her concept in connecting survivors, and she was suddenly watching that power unfold before her very eyes. She also found ways of moving forward her own agendas in this new environment.

The courage to share is only the beginning, and as a longtime advocate, she knew that there should be further action after a victim's public disclosure. Coming forward, she noted, takes courage but could also be followed by guilt and fear. There had to be a next step, and she hoped that even just a fragment of the millions who supported #MeToo at the height of its popularity, would continue to be connected and involved.

Aside from the future of individual #MeToo supporters and participants, Burke also wanted to address underlying social systems that contributed to the problem of sexual harassment and the powerful men who managed to continue engaging in sexual misbehavior. She wanted to go beyond sexual violence, and into issues of social justice that perpetuate such violence. Sexual violence was only the tip of a behemoth iceberg.

"White Feminism"

Actress Alyssa Milano rightly recognized the work of Tarana Burke in another tweet: "*I was just made aware of an earlier #MeToo movement, and the origin story is equal parts heartbreaking and inspiring*," which she posted along with a link to the roots of Burke's movement as written on a page of the JustBeInc. website. She also made sure to reach out and engage with Burke on how they could use their shared voices toward furthering their goals and ideals as women.

It's a classy act, especially as Milano never intended for her tweet to be viral, nor did she ever claim credit for founding the powerful and resonant concept in it. But that she had to rectify an incorrect credit was problematic all on its own, and symptomatic of another problem America has to grapple with – women of color like Tarana Burke and the underserved communities she advocates, simply do not seem to have a voice.

Second wave feminists were concerned with how 'the personal is political,' and this is apparently as true of women's issues as they are of other social justice issues, including race. For its critics, "#MeToo" was overshadowing Burke's original "me too Movement™" the same way "mainstream" feminism has "whitewashed" women's issues. #MeToo in its evolved form has allegedly evolved away from Burke's vision into something white and privileged.

It may be recalled that in the First Wave, racism reared a bit of its ugly, persistent head when African American men got the right to vote well ahead of women. This is therefore not feminism's first rodeo with complex issues of race and from the look of things, it isn't going to be the last.

What women of color face are multiple power systems stemming from both their gender as well as their race. Thus, some allegations will be treated by society more seriously than others. Some accusers will be heard and others, not. There will be larger indignation, media attention and public support for some cases more than others. Some voices will be louder than others. Unfortunately for women of color, this is seldom ever them. This is one of the reasons why the critics of #MeToo fear that the changes it would bring wouldn't necessarily benefit all types of women.

Milano's accidental virulence versus a decade of Tarana Burke's quiet hard work wouldn't be the first time that the call of a privileged white woman is heeded where that of a black woman was not. Some women boycotted Twitter after outspoken actress, Rose McGowan's account was suspended with #WomenBoycottTwitter. But prominent women of color had been silenced and attacked on this and other online platforms too with little public outcry, among them, television and movie star Leslie Jones and ESPN anchor Jemele Hill. Examples like these make some women of color hesitant to back feminist action, especially when white women have not shown themselves to be "allies" in other social justice issues like police brutality. This is why hashtags like #SolidarityIsForWhiteWomen took off; some women of color simply did not feel that white feminists had their backs, when they were all supposed to be fighting social injustice and the structures that kept all of them oppressed. This is also why the term "White Feminist" exists. There are feminists who have privileges of their race that they may not even be aware of.

Actress Emma Watson, a beloved figure in entertainment from her role as the intellectual, courageous and pragmatic Hermione Granger of the groundbreaking *Harry Potter* movies, is a trim, beautiful, straight, young white woman of means, fame and a fine education. She can therefore be considered privileged by most imaginable metrics. The actress is a Goodwill Ambassador for United Nations, and has used her fame for the promotion of women's issues. In spite of all her hard work, she had what some critics called a "blind spot" – the unique experiences of women of color. Watson soon landed the label "white feminist," which she received with panic and confusion. Upon further reflection however, she realized she should have been more aware of the privileges, experiences and perspectives accorded by her color, and her part in perpetuating a *"structurally racist"* system. The introspective actress has been praised for her acknowledgment of the issue, her insightful response, and productive approach in moving forward – she spoke openly of wanting to do better and reaching out to diverse women. Being a feminist, she said, was *"an interrogation of self"* and allowing herself to be called out. She also used her considerable platform to include a reading on racism in *Our Shared Shelf,* her feminist book club.

Divided Feminists?

Like most collectives and organizations of people, feminists experience fissures and fractures. There is after all, no one feminism, just like there is no single type of "woman." Experiences and the views they produce, ideas of how to move forward and the ability to push their respective agendas, differ. Sometimes divisions can even kill momentum.

One of the most interesting and perhaps slightly disappointing divides exposed by #MeToo, are hints of a generational divide between this era's brand of feminism and that of the previous waves. When faced with criticism, for example, one writer called a TV anchor, a *"second-wave-feminist has-been,"* which was a slander on what some perceive as the more moderate feminist views of the older era's professional women, compared to this era's rejection of male entitlement and insensitivity.

Though it of course does not apply to everyone, there are divides on racial lines, age lines, and of course, cultural and ideological lines on hot topics like reproductive choices and religious restrictions on women. For the latter, especially with regard to the Muslim faith, it can be like walking on eggshells – is a particular practice a cultural issue that if challenged can expose the challenger to accusations of racism? Or are some practices and restrictions intrinsically unfair for women and destined for change, as part of the impositions of an oppressive patriarchy? These are indeed fissures that are just as difficult to breach, as religion and ideology are inextricable from cornerstone women's issues like sex education birth control and abortion. Corollary to this is the political divide.

For example - an exit poll with a base of almost 25,000 respondents from the most recent U.S. presidential elections, shared by CNN, showed that while Hillary Clinton secured the majority of the female vote, she beat Trump only by a slim margin. The same could be said of white, college graduate women; Hillary secured 51% to Trump's surprisingly robust 44%. Donald Trump won over white women, at 52% to Hillary's 43%. Non-white women, on the other hand, voted heavily in favor of Hilary Clinton. While elections are complex decisions and not the only signifier of differences, it remains a signpost on a person's view of how his country should look like and how it should solve its myriad problems. Female voters, apparently, were looking at two different Americas. *"Don't forget: White Women Voted for TRUMP,"* said the poster of a woman of color protestor, illustrating one of the puzzling outcomes of an election won by a man with a questionable record on views on and treatment of women.

Later on, experts would weigh in on why this may have been the outcome. White women may have voted along party lines; they are split almost at the half between those who identify as Republican and those who identify as Democrat. The controversial Kellyanne Conway, counselor to President Trump, weighed in too, saying people voted as they usually do – "... *on things that affect them, not just things that offend them.*" Hillary Clinton had a theory too, and a controversial one that still held painful truths. She said that white women vote under pressure from the men in their lives. Some studies back her statement. Single women seemed to vote with a collective "women" in mind, while married women considered the needs of their families first, which were usually tied with their husband's position as breadwinner. If the economics worked for the husband, who would statistically earn more for the family than the woman even if he wasn't the sole breadwinner, then the woman would vote according to that economic interest. Furthermore, pro-woman policies may even be seen as a threat to a husband upon whom the woman depends, if his position is threatened by gender equality in the workplace.

In this sense, 'the personal is political' comes up again; because of the structures that place a woman in a position of dependence on her husband, she can and sometimes will vote against the interests of the larger womanhood. On the other hand, Hillary's loss may be looked at as an important reminder that women weren't simply going to vote another woman into the nation's highest office; even feminists did not necessarily turn up for Clinton, much as they may have wanted a woman in the Oval Office. The vote is a complex choice influenced by many factors that cannot be ignored. Unfortunately, the system is stacked, not just against women *per se*, but through multiple power dynamics that connect to each other.

Another thing that may not have endeared Hillary Clinton to the so-called "women's vote" (the existence of which is debatable) is that there are also questions about whether or not the experiences of elite, white women can really speak for female minorities when they do not share their experiences.

In #MeToo, for example, the elites who suffered sexual harassment may have overshadowed the already-underserved sexual assault victims that inspired the original MeToo campaign to begin with. One of the most concrete plans inspired by #MeToo is #TimesUp, which includes a legal fund for use of women to combat unequal and unsafe work environments. This, however, wouldn't be including a young person of color who is not in the professional work force – the type of young woman whom Tarana Burke championed in the original iteration of her decade-old campaign.

There are really so many points of division. Hopefully, however, these differences are able to lend voice and help each other.

IV. What's Next, and the End Game

"Struggle" is a word often associated to movements seeking change. All struggles have an ending. For feminism however, their cause is a struggle that doesn't simply end. It is either won, or it continues on.

This is why the influential voices of #MeToo had to shift the narrative away from Harvey Weinstein. It's not enough to demonize one man and relegate him to the edges of society, like an ogre on the fringes of an old town with its secrets, as if simply sending him away could solve the problem. Perspectives and solutions had to be systemic.

One of the key differences between Burke's original "Me Too" campaign and "Time's Up" is that the former is about healing, survival and community action in the face of sexual violence. It was a more personal approach. Time's Up, on the other hand, is more about a healthy workplace and access to employment opportunities. Time's Up involves prominent Hollywood women including Academy Award winners Reese Witherspoon and Natalie Portman, and television queen Shonda Rimes. Time's Up fights for workplaces that are free of harassment, assault and discrimination. They are premised on solving the inequality that underlies harassment, because power imbalance is conducive to predatory behavior. They aim to do this through policy and legislation, and are looking at means to penalize companies that turn a blind eye to harassment, or resort to non-disclosure agreements to silence victims.

In a nutshell, #MeToo is personal and anecdotal. #TimesUp slants to objective and political, toward the creation of systems that don't rely on off-the-cuff firings and apologies from transgressors and those that employ and empower them. This is an example of how different views and approaches give feminism energy and dynamism.

Perhaps the things that unite are more powerful than the things that divide… and as proven by history, when women are united, they are hard to deny.